# FORGED

AMANDA BACH

www.TrueVinePublishing.org

Forged
Amanda Bach

Published by
True Vine Publishing Co.
810 Dominican Dr.
Nashville, TN 37228
www.TrueVinePublishing.org


ISBN: 978-1-968092-77-1 Paperback
ISBN: 978-1-968092-78-8 eBook



Printed in the United States of America—First printing.

## DISCLAIMER

This book is intended for informational and inspirational purposes only. The content reflects the author's personal experiences, perspectives, and research and is not intended to substitute professional advice of any kind, including medical, psychological, or financial guidance. Readers are encouraged to consult with a qualified professional before making any decisions related to their health, wellness, or lifestyle.

All stories and examples shared in this book are either based on personal experience or have been altered for privacy. Any resemblance to actual persons, living or dead, is purely coincidental and unintentional.

Results discussed or implied in this book are not guaranteed. Each individual's journey is unique, and outcomes will vary based on personal circumstances, consistency, and commitment.

By reading this book, you acknowledge that you are responsible for your own choices, actions, and results. The author assumes no responsibility for any outcomes resulting from the use or application of the information provided.

Also here our my picture.  Use the headshot for the back cover (feel free to crop out all of the dead space at the top) and put the picture of the family on the last page of the book.

# Table of Contents

# One Woman's Story

What if the life you're living isn't the one you were meant for? What if the fear, the self-doubt, and the pain you've carried aren't who you are, but what you've learned to believe?

From a life driven by fear to one rooted in love, this book is your invitation to awaken to the truth of who you are. It is designed to guide you in transforming your life by becoming aware of your thought patterns, because once you do, everything begins to change. When we shift our awareness, we shift our reality. Negative thinking no longer controls us, and we begin to step into a state of peace, clarity, and emotional freedom.

As human beings, we are wired to grow, to heal, and to rise. Yet from a young age, many of us carry invisible wounds. I know this firsthand. I struggled with deep feelings of unworthiness and feeling unloved, even when no one was directly to blame, but your past does not define you.

We all carry experiences that shape us, and as we grow older, unresolved traumas can resurface and play out in our daily lives. The question is, will you continue to live in cycles, or will you choose to break free?

In Part One, I take you through my personal journey, the pain, the awakening, and the transformation. In Part Two, you'll find practical steps to begin your own healing journey. You'll learn how to align with your true self and with God, the Creator. You'll discover how to raise your vibration, reclaim your power, and step fully into a life of purpose. Most importantly, you will learn how to love and heal yourself. The life you've been searching for… has been within you all along.

# PART I

# Childhood Memories

My earliest memories take me back to 1986. I was just two years old. I remember crying in the back seat of the car while waving goodbye to my mom. She was in a halfway house at the time. In 1985, she went to prison for first-degree burglary and assault to do deadly harm. That carried a twenty five year prison sentence in the state of Iowa. She was protecting my sister.

Flashback to the night my sister and I were getting babysat, while my mom was out on the town. The babysitter dropped us off the next morning, about 3:30 am, and my mom arrived home shortly after. Later that morning, my grandma was cooking pancakes. My mom was bathing my sister, and she realized she had bruises all over her head and chunks of hair falling out. She was completely healthy prior to that night.

My mom immediately called CPS to investigate. Due to her living in Florida at the time, CPS would no longer continue the investigation. Eighteen months after the abuse, my mom, back in Iowa, was at a bar. She saw the babysitter's cousin and asked where the girl lived. Mom and her friend were drunk and decided to take a trip to her house. She wanted to talk about that night she was supposed to be taking care of us, but dropped us off with new bruises and scars.

She knocked on the door, and the woman's boyfriend opened it, closing it almost immediately after realizing who it was. They never came to see what mom wanted. My mom tells me today that was all she needed to know before deciding to bust the door down. She pulled the phone wires out of the wall and beat her head off the toilet for abusing my sister. When the cops arrived, she stepped outside with her hands behind her back and said, "I'm here to settle a score." She hit the first page of the Nonpareil newspaper in Council Bluffs, Iowa. That was the only thing said in all her paperwork.

When battling this case, she later found that my sister's abuser was pregnant at the time and had a miscarriage. She was now possibly facing manslaughter charges. It was later determined that the miscarriage happened 68 hours prior to my mom arriving at her house. God was in complete control and knew why my mom did what she did. Eventually, it was found that the lady was abusing her own son. He burned her house down. The pictures of my sister were the only thing that gave my mom grace, and God, of course.

After my mom went to prison, my dad, on paper (my sister's biological dad), got custody of my sister and I. It was the second memory I have. We lived in Florida at the time, and I would get scolded for crying in the bedroom for missing my mom. We were surrounded by feces, and ate so much government cheese that I still cannot fathom eating it today. We would roll the cheese into balls and eat it. When my mom finally got custody back, we arrived with scabies and were filthy.

"I was facing twenty five years," she said. "At first, I pleaded to a first-degree charge, but they eventually reduced it to a second degree, which carried fifteen years. In the end, I survived and served eighteen months and spent five years on paper," she continued. "After that, I was able to get all my rights back and move forward with my life, and with you girls."

When my mom finally put the pieces back together, she was living with my biological father. From my young perspective, everything seemed perfect. My mom kept the house neat and warm, and we lived in a quiet, safe neighborhood. As we all learn, appearances can be deceiving. Never judge a book by its cover. It was a time that now feels like a distant dream. A time when kids played outside until the streetlights flickered on. Another life when summer nights were spent chasing fireflies and swimming in the lake, and playing in the sprinkler.

Being that little girl, weaving flowers into crowns, completely immersed in the magic of childhood. The first five years while living with my dad were amazing. I felt like I was finally home. The movie nights, the beautiful Christmases, believing in Santa. As kids, we could not ask for more. Even in those moments of innocence, deeper stories were beginning to unfold beneath the surface.

My first experience with religion came in childhood. From the ages five to ten, I attended Awana every Wednesday night, thanks to my best friend at the time, who would bring me along. It was during those years that I began forming a connection with a higher power, with God. I have fond memories of camping trips, dinners at nice restaurants, playing with the neighborhood kids and just enjoying being a kid. I remember our dogs and how much I loved them. I would come home from school, and they would be in the driveway waiting for me. Every Halloween, my mom would make sure we had the best costumes, skipping home with pillow cases full of candy, and the way my mom loved us fiercely, with everything she had.

My father struggled with alcoholism, but it wasn't just drinking; it was the rage, the unpredictability, the way fear threaded through our home. The man who should have protected us often became the source of our pain, and still, she loved him. She loved him through the brokenness, through the nights that felt endless and unsafe. I can't explain it; it wasn't rational. It was survival, it was hope, it was a kind of love that demanded every ounce of her strength. That's the man I called father.

From grappling with bullying at school, because of my weight, and then coming home not knowing what to expect, my perception of that man began to change. Behind closed doors, our home was filled with fear and violence. Every argument between my parents ended with my mom being hurt. My sister and I would run to the neighbor's house when the fighting started; it was our safe place. We knew that once we got there, the police would soon arrive.

Part of our lives became that routine. The moments we would not want to be alone with my dad because he scared us. The times he would grab my shoulder so hard that my mom would have to take me to the hospital. It became so bad that I had a pinched nerve from it. I carry those experiences with me every day and have built relationships with my then neighbors over the years. One of my best friends is an esthetician. She would babysit my sister and I when my mom and dad would go out during those times. We became close, and I watched her build a business of her own and struggle through her own issues. She knows who she is if she is reading this.

The helplessness I felt as a child was overwhelming. I'll never forget seeing my mother pinned against the wall by her neck. What made it worse was seeing the beating that left a dent in the drywall and a deeper scar on our hearts. My dad would lure me to the bathroom in the morning while he was on the toilet, and I would sit on the floor in the corner. I have my assumptions now and know that darker forces from generations were at play. The cycles rooted through my entire family. My father betraying my mom was the final breaking point.

He chased my mother down the driveway with an axe. I remember that night like it had been set on fire in my mind. We sat frozen in the car, windows rolled up, hearts pounding in our ears. The gravel crunched under his boots with every step. The cold night air smelled of alcohol and fear. She had to defend herself. Not long after, my mom went to jail for nearly killing him.

"Get in the house! Hurry!" My mother shouted, her voice sharp and trembling.

"Mom don't," I started, but my words caught in my throat as I watched through the bedroom window. She gunned the engine, tires spinning on the pavement. My stomach dropped when she aimed the car through the garage, toward him. I saw red. No, she saw red. She hit him while he sat on his Harley in the garage.

He went down, unconscious, and the garage smelled of gasoline and burnt rubber. The flashing lights hit us, blue and red, cutting through the night like the knives he wore on his belt. I could hear sirens wailing. The air tingled as I could feel the adrenaline thrumming through my chest. It tasted harsh like the metallic tang of blood on my tongue. That night, everything shattered, and nothing felt the same.

She ended up going to jail that night, but the judge showed her a small mercy. They knew the story, every call she'd made over the years reporting beatings, the abuse, the nights of terror. They saw the pattern, and for once, someone acknowledged that she had been fighting to survive.

After that, his family turned away. They wanted nothing to do with us, and just like that, I lost my grandparents on my father's side. The doors closed, the phone went silent, and I've had no contact with them since. It left a hollow ache. A sense of being cut loose from part of my own history. We were forced to navigate the pain and the absence on our own.

It wasn't until I grew up that I truly began to understand the depth of the damage. I saw how easily trauma passes from one generation to the next. My first cousin on my mom's side, the eldest of the boys, would molest me with my clothes on when I was a kid. At that age, I did not know it was wrong, but I knew deep down something was not right.

I completely disassociated until I was old enough to heal and understand how disturbing it was. I also realized I had a choice. I chose to break the cycle. I chose to create a different life for my children, one built on healing, love, and freedom, waking each day with a peaceful heart. A life living authentically, loving deeply without fear, and moving through the world guided by truth. Always having gratitude, and the quiet joy of simply being. I understood as I got older that I had to be the one to break the chains. I had to take my power back. It was not only for myself, but for my kids, for the generations before me.

I remember my Aunt telling me that I was different from the rest. I was going to do something great, and I had a calling and a light about me. I never understood it then, but I fully understand it now. God's purpose is always higher than our own, even if we don't see it at the time. He chose me, because he knew I was going to be the one breaking the cycles from all the generations before me.

After my mom and dad split up, life became a blur of movement and uncertainty. We never stayed in one place for too long. Just as I'd start to get comfortable, we were packing up again. I remember feeling like I didn't belong anywhere. The ground could shift beneath me at any moment. It left me with a deep sense of instability, and even deeper, a quiet desperation to survive. I think that's why, as an adult, I've worked so hard to give my own children the very thing I never had: stability, a safe home, consistency, something they could count on.

When I was ten, I met some of the closest friends I would ever know. My mom was battling the separation from my dad and trying to make it on her own. I was growing up, living in the inner city, trying to find myself. Those friends became family. We would do everything together in a little part of Omaha, Nebraska, the South side of Dodge Street.

The summers, the late nights, the first crushes, and my first cigarette. That is when I understood that everyone was going through something, and just because you are going through something, does not make anyone else's situation any less. Fearing for my life, being chased down the street with a chain, and those friends who were the only ones there, had my back. There was more to fear. Even during this time, I never knew my best friend's dad was molesting her, not till I got older.

My childhood memories take me back to that part of the city, on the north side of Dodge Street, where life had its own rough edges and hidden stories that were both ordinary and unforgettable. Getting my bike stolen was the tip of the iceberg while living in Hillside apartments, listening to the kids next door screaming because they were getting beaten by their parents. Walking from one end of town to the next. My first kiss. Sitting in Gifford Park late at night before getting pulled over by the cops for drinking alcohol at the ripe age of thirteen, I wondered what my mom would say. That was life, and you did not question it; you just rolled with it. Back then, it was raw and real, and if you did not know how to fight, you did not know how to survive.

Those days were crazier than they needed to be. Partying with men who were twice our age, sometimes not even remembering how I got home. Being so wasted, I pulled down my pants in the middle of the grocery aisle to go pee, and then fell over laughing with one of my best friends because we couldn't find the bathroom. Drinking 40's and cruising the city streets, knowing you should be home getting ready for school the next day. Watching your fourteen year-old friends have babies in junior high and somehow that was all normal and the status quo. I remember sitting in silence sometimes. I watched the world around me and felt this pull in my chest. It felt like my life was meant to go somewhere beyond what I could see. I couldn't explain it, but I knew deep down that the story being written for me wasn't finished yet. I just did not know what it was until I got much older.

We lived on Park Ave, and Hinky Dink was the supermarket my mom worked at. I remember our door being kicked in, because my mom was involved with drugs. Being followed by men in black suits to school and to the payphone. Writing to boys in group homes, not knowing they would become some of the best people I know and have my back whenever I need them. I had a pager, and it was definitely an experience. Every cool kid had them, and I was one of them.

My sister was fifteen and had started seeing a man who was here illegally. She met him through my cousin, and my mom was not fond of the situation. When my sister fell in love with him, mom really did not have a choice.

He was running drugs for his cousins, and looking back, I truly believe that the world swallowed her whole. Mom was introduced to his cousins when they showed up at our house one night, and she was just getting off of work. She told them to, "get the fuck out of my house." Little did she know, she would need them to help with her drug activities too. As my sister evolved her relationship with her boyfriend, my mom grew her relationship with his cousins.

He hurt her in ways we didn't fully understand at the time. One day, he then, just like that, vanished. He was there, and the next he was gone. By the time he was done, he had left her dismantled, emotionally destroyed, and trying to rebuild herself from the pieces he had broken. He wasn't just anyone; he was her first love, the person she trusted most. A shell of the sister I had known. It was heartbreaking to witness. To watch my only sister go through such a traumatic experience and not be able to do anything about it. It stung.

Part of me was lost. Part of me thinks he harmed her intentionally, to scare her into silence. A silence to keep her from exposing whatever it was they were doing. Whatever the reason, the damage was done. Something inside her broke, and she was never the same. Her mental health declined fast. One minute she was with us, and the next, she'd disappear into oblivion.

My mom and I would spend hours searching, driving through neighborhoods, scanning the streets, hoping to find her before something terrible happened. Sometimes we'd find her walking alone on the side of the road, or even in the middle of a highway, her face blank and distant, like she was somewhere far away that we couldn't reach.

There were nights she would stand over my bed while I slept, holding a knife in her hand. I would wake up to the sound of her heavy breathing in the dark; my heart would pound so hard. I grieved for my sister, and she was still alive. I mourned for the sister I grew up with, and was angry and bitter towards the man who caused it. I didn't know what to do, how to react, or who to turn to. I was just a kid, still a minor myself, trying to hold my world together while everything around me was falling apart. I wanted control. I yearned for emotional support and stability.

Years later, my sister was finally diagnosed with schizophrenia, after countless years of my mom searching desperately for the right diagnosis. She had been on the wrong medication for so long, and all the while, I watched my sister slowly fade away. I remember the day I saw those pill capsules in a glass and didn't question it. I wish I had. I wish I had trusted that uneasy feeling in my gut and confronted what was really happening.

The nights she would be in the basement, and I would not see her. I would never question going to see if she was okay. She was so cut off from society. He consumed her and everything she did. The times he would get mad at her and be mean, and I would brush it off and act like it was nothing. When you come from a hurt place in life, you think stuff like that is normal.

Looking back at my earlier childhood with my dad and mom, I completely overlooked the fact that my sister's boyfriend was being abusive towards her. It's hard to write about the memories because it raises many weighted emotions and brings tears to my eyes, only if I could have done something different.

My sister spent too much time in the basement with that man. We never imagined the worst. The truth, when it finally surfaced, was darker than any of us had pictured. My sister had been date-raped by him and his brother. When the words were finally spoken out loud, everything went silent.

It was the kind of silence that presses against your body, concealing you in its own bubble and steals the air from your lungs. My mother just sat there, her face pale, shaking her head as if refusing to believe that something so cruel could have happened under our own roof. I remember feeling a mix of anger, heartbreak, and helplessness all at once. Like the ground beneath our family had suddenly cracked open into the molten core of the earth.

At that moment, none of us knew what to say. There were tears, long pauses, and the quiet understanding that nothing about our lives would feel the same again. Even in the shock and pain, there was something else there too, an unspoken instinct to protect her, to hold each other closer and somehow find a way forward together. She had to undergo an abortion in order to take the medication she needed to care for herself. She didn't finish high school. She fell just eight credits short of graduation, but she is a survivor. She truly has the heart of a fighter.

She was no longer the sister I grew up with, the one who played tag while camping, raced bikes, mom braiding her hair in the mornings, or ran through the neighborhood with friends. Our lives had changed forever. She was no longer the sister I would want to be, who had long black hair and was considered a "prep". As I have grown and watched everything she has endured, I'm more in admiration of her than I have ever been. I will always look up to my sister. She has fought countless battles that would destroy some people.

My mom worked long, exhausting hours, mornings from ten to two, then back again from four to ten as a cocktail waitress. That's how she raised us, with grit and determination. We lived on Jaynes Street in North Omaha.

I was fourteen then, caught up in my own struggles with school and friends. Going between Jaynes and 28th and Croby. I was attacked in my front yard because my best friend was seeing a man that some other girl was with.

They ran into my house. We were all drinking underage, but that is how the story goes. The only thing that saved me that night was a friend running up the street to pull them off me. Although I held my own, it was not a fair fight, and I had to defend myself. The brawls in the middle of the street, watching my best friend's tooth get knocked out. It sucked waking up with your room full of toilet paper, because the coolest kids rolled your room when you fell asleep first at your party. It all went by so fast, and it seems like a lifetime ago.

We thought this was typical and maybe it was to us at the time. It was how we grew up, and it was not for the frail. It was a rush and all the same, a path in the wrong direction. Even though we were young, we had to stay strong. We grew up in the hood. Those are some of the best memories I have.

The connections I made in the most urban areas of the city shaped who I have become. When you know someone who can drop a beat and make a whole flow out of nothing, it is inspiring. You knew that it was meant for a greater destiny.

Riding down Ames and watching the cars with big rims and flashy paint jobs. Sitting in the Time Out parking lot waiting in line for the best fried chicken and strawberry soda you'll ever try. The BBQs you would attend with some of the best food. It was a time to be alive and some of the scariest moments.

When my best friend and I were chilling by Louis supermarket and heard a drive by literally the next block over - *Pop, pop, pop, pop*! The dread I felt take over me was something I will never forget. It swallowed me whole and took over my body. We listened to them turn the block, slowly cruising down the street with their lights off. We quickly ducked into our seats, adrenaline taking over, praying we would see our kids and that this wasn't going to be our last night alive. That was city life, understanding fight or flight mode from a very early age. If you know, you just know.

My mom, of course, blamed herself and withdrew emotionally after what happened to my sister. She became distant and coped with drugs. In the end, she lost the guardianship of her. My grandmother and aunt didn't believe mom was capable of caring for her. My sister was in and out of medical facilities. Some were assisted living, and some were independent. It was hard to watch knowing that she was alone when we had to leave.

There was a void in my heart. A deep hollow, I couldn't fill, no matter how hard I tried. I felt like my reality had shifted in an instant, and nothing around me felt safe or familiar anymore. I constantly wondered if she was okay. Was she safe? Were the people around her trustworthy? This trauma was one that settled in slowly, heavily, and quietly. I started to understand that the world is not as safe as I once believed it to be.

My mom was the black sheep of the family because of her own issues as a child. Starting with her grandfather molesting her and the entire family sweeping it under the rug. In the summer of 1976, my mother would spend days at her grandmother's house like any other summer. My mother loved spending time with her grandfather. There was something about those quiet afternoons with him that felt safe and steady, like time slowed down.

One warm summer afternoon, with the sun hanging heavy in the sky, he looked over at her and said, "Come ride with me. I need to run to the store to grab some milk." While they were driving, she noticed that they drove past the store and started towards Hummel Park. When they arrived, he parked the truck and started to fondle her and kiss her. She was totally freaked out and did not know what to do.

My grandma was in Louisiana on a shrimp boat when she received the call from my mom. That night, she snuck to the phone when everyone was in bed, scared and wanting to confide in her own mother. When she picked up the phone and heard the news, she told my mom that she would be there as soon as possible. My grandma immediately traveled back to Carter Lake, Iowa, and walked in with a gun in her car. She sat at the kitchen table and told my great-grandmother that they needed to talk. My grandma's words - "I outta blow your fucking head off."

My mom never went back after that. We, kids, were not allowed there until after my great-grandfather died. Once we got older, we knew that it was deeper than that. My great-grandfather molested a lot of the women in my family. My grandma and her sister went and lived with my great-great-grandmother because of it. They were dropped off with suitcases, and it was hidden.

This was the reason we never went to see my great-grandmother in Carter Lake. My mom never gave up. Despite battling addiction herself, she fought relentlessly to bring my sister home. Today, my mom and sister are doing well. They live together and truly care for one another.

They are family, so it warms my heart to see their bond and how it has grown. I love them endlessly. I draw my strength from my mom. I wouldn't be the woman I am today without her. Every mistake she made, she did her best with what she had. I will always be thankful for her and what she has taught me.

My mom showed me what perseverance really looks like, even in the moments when life tried to break her. She carried more than most people could ever imagine. She still found a way to love, and to keep going, and to hold our family together. Watching her fight through everything taught me resilience, compassion, and the kind of courage that doesn't always look loud, but never gives up. She is the most caring, understanding, and beautiful soul I know, with a heart of gold. All she has ever wanted, and deserved, is to be loved.

Isn't that what we all deserve?

After what happened to my sister, everything changed. I was in high school, still trying to figure out who I was. Funny enough, in many ways, I'm still searching for her. Growth isn't something that just happens; it's a lifelong process. As we get older, we start peeling back the layers of our lives and begin to understand who we are as individuals, truly. We recognize the traumas we've experienced, learn healthier ways to cope, and, most importantly, gain control over our emotions.

We stop making excuses and begin making decisions that reflect our values and morals, the truths we choose to stand on. Deep down, we all know the difference between right and wrong. That inner voice, our conscience, reminds us. Despite centuries of debate, there's still no universally agreed-upon theory of consciousness (Falk, 2023). Somehow, we instinctively know when we're aligned, or misaligned, with our higher selves. We know the difference between right and wrong, even when we choose to do poorly.

*"We choose our joys and sorrows long before we experience them."*

*~Khalil Gibran*

# Motherhood

I had my first daughter at 17, and I wasn't ready. I didn't know what I was doing, and I was terrified. I felt completely alone, especially given the situation with my mom and my sister. My mother was struggling with addiction and the trauma related to my sister, and it was more than I could process at the time. The moment I told her I was pregnant, she was lying in bed, furious. That reaction stayed with me.

We were living in a run-down townhouse with drug users coming in and out of the complex. Throwing up from morning sickness and still forcing myself to get up and go to school with no guidance. The father of my daughter wanted nothing to do with us. I believe he held resentment for a long time and still does, especially after I had to put him on child support, much-needed, just to qualify for state assistance. I didn't have help, and I had to withstand it. Welfare and food stamps became part of my life.

My oldest daughter's father still has no contact with her and has never put in the effort to try. He has always known my number and where we lived. The questions remain in her head: why does he have a relationship with his other children, but not her? That is something I have had to let go and understand that it is a reflection on his character and has nothing to do with her or me. She knows she is loved and will always know she is enough.

December 2nd, 2001, I gave birth at 1:38 pm after 16 long hours of labor. Only one person came to visit me in the hospital. When it was time to leave, I drove myself home in a car that could only be started with a screwdriver. My mom had dropped it off for me. On the drive home, the car broke down. No one came to help, so I flagged down an older couple who kindly picked us up and drove us home. Back to chaos, a townhouse full of tension and pain. A mother on drugs, a sister battling mental health issues, and me, a brand new mother with no roadmap and no support.

There was no peace, no direction. What I do remember is having the greatest friends I could ask for. They got me through some of the hardest times of my life. I will always carry them with me, even if we are miles apart. Those same friends would go through some of the worst hardships of their lives, but make it out and become some of the most successful people I know. One of those friends whom I particularly looked up to, helped me navigate the system. She showed me how to apply for WIC and state aid. She guided me through the fragile, early days of motherhood, uplifting me when everything felt new and overwhelming.

I was still learning how to find my footing as a young mother, but she was there helping me stand. It wasn't the perfect support, but it was what I had. I'm grateful in my own way. I even remember her teaching me little tricks, like adding cereal to the formula so the baby would sleep a little longer. She taught me so much, not just about motherhood, but about life. If you're reading this now, thank you.

I missed the entire first semester of my senior year, but I refused to give up. I went to night school during the second semester and graduated with my class on time, despite all the odds stacked against me. After graduation, I had my second child, a boy. He is, and will forever be my ace. He has been through some of the hardest moments with me and is still thriving in life. Unfortunately, my relationship with his father was just as toxic and unhealthy as my first. I spent five years chasing him while he messed around on me. I chased meaningless relationships with people who were not good for me, because I did not know my worth.

I did not believe that I deserved to be loved. When I was broken, I lost control of my own thoughts and feelings, and I attracted exactly what I feared the most. When I was clinging to something so tightly, I ended up losing that very thing. It's not an easy concept to process or understand. When it finally clicks, the truth of it settles in, and it feels like an awakening. It feels like an unexpected and powerful epiphany. I began to understand that some things were never meant to be forced, only experienced. That love, people, and moments in life were meant to flow freely, not gripped with fear of losing them.

In that realization, something inside me softened. I stopped chasing. I stopped grasping. I simply allowed what was meant to stay… and trust that what isn't will find its way out. I know now that you are the love you give, and that is enough.

Have you ever felt like you lost control of yourself because life didn't unfold the way you hoped? That was me. I pursued my son's father, desperately searching for my worth, trying to understand what I had done wrong and why he didn't want me. I couldn't make sense of why he lied, cheated, and had children with other women. The question that repeated in my head was always the same: Why am I not enough? Looking back, the pattern is clear. My father and his choices, my mother and hers, my oldest daughter's father, my son's father, and so on.

The same threads are woven through different people and different moments in time. Different faces, different circumstances, but somehow the same lessons return again and again. For a long time, I couldn't see it. When you're living inside the storm, everything feels random, like life is just happening to you. The distance has a way of sharpening the truth. Time pulls the curtain back, and suddenly, the connections are impossible to ignore.

Over and over, I manifested the same cycle of feeling unworthy and undeserving of love. Everyone I cared about seemed to fail me. How could they possibly care about my feelings? Did they even realize the ripple effect their choices had on my life? Did I even understand the choices I made, and the ripple effect they had?

I began to understand that patterns don't repeat themselves for no reason. They return until something inside of you changes, until you recognize what you've been tolerating, what you have been accepting, and what you've been unconsciously drawn to. It once felt familiar. Once you see it clearly, really see it, you can't unsee it. That's when the real work begins, deciding whether the story continues the same as it always has, or whether it finally changes with you.

*"Children are like wet cement: whatever falls on them makes an impression."*

*~Haim Ginott*

# The Church & Adoption

At twenty, I moved out of my mother's home. I was young, with two small children, and had no clear direction. Thankfully, I was offered a place to live by a woman from my church. The children's pastor. She took me in, mentored me, and in many ways, molded me into the professional I am today. She knows who she is, and I will always be grateful for what she poured into me. I lived with her from April 2005 until March 2006.

By twenty two, I had moved into my first apartment with my kids. I adored them. Every decision I made centered on giving them the life I never had. I continued attending church faithfully on Wednesday, Saturday, and Sunday. We never missed a service. I was dedicated, I served, I cleaned that building from top to bottom more times than I could count.

I contributed to the Pastor and his wife. My kids spent time with their kids on multiple occasions. They would encourage me to whip my kids because that is how they did things; it was disturbing and influenced. It was always, "Spare the rod and spoil the child." I would feel guilty at times when I disciplined them and could have handled it differently.

As a single mom, I made sure to set aside time for the kids. Every Friday night, we would go to the laundromat, rent movies from Blockbuster, and order chinese at the Rice Bowl. It's a memory we will never forget. A memory they will never forget. They are such nostalgic moments.

At the time, I believed I had found a place of refuge, a safe space. Looking back, I realized it was anything but safe. I am grateful for the faith I have now and the spiritual family I've found since. What I experienced in my early twenties was a system more focused on control than compassion. The Church is supposed to be a sanctuary for the broken and the seeking. It took me years to understand that not all churches operate with the heart of God. Some function more like businesses, concerned with image, money, and power. That's not freedom; that is only manipulation.

I remember being unable to pay my tithes. I was a single mother, doing everything I could to keep my head above water. When I explained that I didn't qualify for financial assistance because I made "too much" to receive state aid, but not enough to cover my expenses, I was reprimanded. I was told that not paying tithes went against God's word. What kind of faith community tears down someone who's reaching out for help?

I asked for assistance from the very church I had poured so much of myself into. I was faithful, and I served, but when I needed support, I was treated like a burden. They looked at me as if I were lazy, abusing the system. I had worked hard to become independent, and I was proud of that, but even then, I still struggled.

A couple of times, I fell behind on rent and had to reach out to other churches, strangers, for help. My own church never showed up for me. That feeling, of being judged and diminished by people who claim to represent love and grace. It's something I won't forget. The church became a place where I felt small, shamed, and inferior, and no one, no matter their mistakes, should ever be made the topic of a sermon. When leaders position themselves above others, it's a red flag. One I wish I had seen sooner.

Before my marriage in 2010, I met a man at the church in 2006, one of the leaders. We began dating in secret. He was fifteen years older than me. It wasn't something I planned, and neither was the pregnancy that followed. I think we were both just searching for something to hold on to. Something that felt real. When I told him I was pregnant, he wanted nothing to do with it.

The church elders called a meeting. We both sat before them, and in that moment, when honesty and accountability mattered most, he turned on me. He said he was a victim of my wrongdoing. I was stunned, betrayed, and once again, alone. The times we spent together, the nights I would go to his house and cook for him. I was hoping and searching for love outside of myself, not realizing what it would cost. The universe will continue to allow toxic patterns in your life until you finally recognize it, and are ready to do the work to evolve. Until you are up for it and willing to surrender, you will continue to seek outside of yourself rather than the love you already have within yourself.

He was excommunicated and never returned to the church. I stayed, sitting in that room with shame heavy on my shoulders, fear in my heart, and a child growing inside me. I knew the truth deep down. I wasn't ready to raise another child. I tried. I brought him home, but eventually, I made one of the hardest decisions of my life: I placed him for adoption. I questioned that decision and went back and forth with it for days after leaving the hospital.

I took him home for twenty four hours, and prayed for understanding and with my entire heart. I understood in those final moments that God had a bigger plan than I did, and I had to release control. The adoptive mom could not have children of her own. God knew they were meant to raise him. I had to surrender and trust that God knew what I did not. It was not a decision made out of weakness, but out of love.

A love so deep and selfless that I chose what was best for him, not what was easiest for me. He came from my body, my blood, but I was not the one chosen to raise him. God had other plans. The adoption is an open adoption, and the parents are better than I could ever hope for. They were there and cut the cord the day he was born. They have raised him to be the most amazing man.

As I watch from afar, I hope he knows how much I love him. That I never stopped loving him and that I always pray for him. There is not a day that goes by that I don't think about him. He will always be a part of me. I will always carry him with me, no matter how far away he is. That will always be one of the most selfless things I have ever done.

After the adoption in January of 2008, I met my husband in August of that same year. The church refused to bless our union. However, God knew what I did not. I know now, and it was one of the hardest lessons I have learned. I was a member for seven years. The Sunday I left, I was mocked from the pulpit, preached about, and humiliated. Who does that to someone seeking love, growth, and healing?

Over the years, I've learned not to question everything. I've learned that sometimes, peace comes not from knowing, but from accepting. Although my path hasn't been easy, it's mine. I've found strength in the very places I once felt shattered. I have found a church family that has opened its arms. They have reminded me of what love is and how important it is to have that support around you.

Listening to older folks around you can provide so much wisdom. Being surrounded by that is something I deeply cherish. There's a certain comfort in it, a grounding feeling that's hard to explain unless you've experienced it. Sitting quietly and hearing the stories of people who have lived entire lifetimes before you. The way their voices carry memories of another time, another way of living. God has shown up and shown out in places where all hope seemed lost. God reminds me that I'm not alone. That I'm whole within myself, within Him, and the more I align and surrender, the more I understand that God has a greater plan.

*"The great art of learning is to understand but little at a time."*

*~ John Locke*

# Marriage, Family & Betrayal

After the adoption was finalized in January 2008, my life began heading down a path I never anticipated.

In August of that year, I reconnected with a friend from high school, the man who would soon become my husband. At the time, I felt a sense of liberation, as if I had closed a painful chapter and was stepping into a new beginning. I was working on my financial stability, determined to move forward.

What I believed was a new beginning slowly unraveled into something I never expected. The hope I carried into the future, the belief that things would finally be different, began to fade piece by piece. Looking back, I realize I was intuitive, but I ignored the signs. Before we even began our relationship, I had a dream about him, a warning from the universe to run. Instead, I ran straight toward him. I didn't know he had an addiction; he hid it for years.

I would soon find him late at night in the kitchen with broken pieces of light bulbs, later understanding this is what he would smoke meth on. He would come home from DJing at bars with powder on his nose. I watched the man I loved destroy himself for instant gratification. I learned the hard truth: no one can make a person with an addiction stop; it has to come from within. Red flags surrounded me, but I stayed.

We married in September 2010.

Deep down, I knew then that it was not right. The wedding was not easy, and nothing went as planned. I was alone the night before the wedding, decorating the reception hall while he was out partying with his friends. I never even got a bachelorette party. The morning of, I was the one who had to go and get the flower girl's hair done, getting them prepared to throw flowers down the aisle. It was not an easy task while I felt the heaviness of the world on my shoulders.

He was happy and oblivious to how I was truly feeling. I was exhausted the day of the ceremony, depleted. Although a woman's wedding day is a complex mix of emotions, I should've been experiencing more of the brighter end of that spectrum. It was in my bones, in my breath, in the quiet spaces between my thoughts. The weight of everything I had already endured sat heavily on my chest. I wasn't sure I made the right choice, and I think my family knew that maybe this wasn't going to end in a lifelong union as well.

Not long after we were married, I gave birth to my youngest child in May of 2011 and that September, I enrolled in college for my business degree. The day I found out I was pregnant, we were sitting in a courtroom facing eviction. I remember how the air felt thick, unmoving, like even breathing took effort. Deep down, before anything was confirmed, I already knew.

My body had been trying to tell me. The quiet nausea in the mornings… the heaviness I could not explain. When it became real, when there was no more guessing, I cried. Not softly, not gracefully, but from a place that had been holding too much for too long. Three years before, I had given up my third child for adoption, and that kind of surrender… it doesn't leave you. It lingers. It reshapes you. It lives quietly in the background of every new beginning.

When I realized I was carrying life again, it didn't feel real; it felt derealized. Not because I did not love her, but because I knew her father would not be there for me. That knowledge did not come from fear of the future. It came from the fear of the red flags I saw. She was the best thing that came out of our marriage, and has brought so much joy to my life.

After we were evicted from my apartment, we made a decision to move in with his great great-grandparents. They were the ones who raised him, and while we had no choice but to move in with his family, there was a sense of uncertainty. His great great-grandmother was battling dementia, and his great great-grandfather grappled with alcoholism. I had this immense perception in my spirit that I should not have married him.

During the pregnancy, my fears came into fruition. Like the beer being spilled over my head in the living room, cold, humiliating, intentional. The night he locked me out of the house, as I stood outside in the cold waiting, wondering how I had become someone that could allow this behavior. His words were sharp and careless, meant to cut. Threats that weren't just about betrayal, but about breaking me down until I believed I deserved it. I felt so alone. Not just physically, but in a way that made me feel disconnected from everything... even myself.

I couldn't even visit my own mom without it turning into an argument or debate. Without tension, without distress, without him making it about control. So I adjusted, I made myself smaller, quieter. I learned how to move carefully inside a life that no longer felt like mine.

There are moments that come to mind now that I still can't fully explain. The premonition while I stood in the kitchen, everything muting around me, as if I was floating outside of myself. Something in me shifted. Not loudly, but clearly, it felt like I was being guided by a power bigger than me. Like something deeper than thought was finally showing me the truth I had avoided to see. I could intuit it, even when I could not prove it.

The burden wasn't mine, but the darkness I had been standing in. The shadows attached to him that I had unknowingly been carrying, showing me the entities that were affixed to him. The nights my oldest daughter would call me while I was in school, feeling something was off, but not listening to my intuition.

In April 2012, we finally got our own place. For the first time, it felt like things were coming into alignment, but there was something I didn't know that would shatter me to my core. This truth would change the dynamic of my entire family in a matter of seconds. It would change the destination of our course in the years to come. Everything shifted, and although it was chaos, it taught me so many lessons that I learned to alchemize.

Only a month after moving into our new home, my oldest daughter handed me a note. In it, she revealed what no mother ever wants to read: my husband had been molesting her for the past eight months. He would bribe her and make my son go upstairs and take showers while he lured her to the basement. He would make her put a robe on, rub lotion on her, and penetrate her with his fingers. Sneak into her room that she shared with her brother, deep into the night, to touch her. She was only nine years old. At that moment, my world collapsed. I hugged my daughter immediately and called the police. I called my husband while he was at work and demanded answers. I was numb and distraught. Trapped.

My daughter was sent to be interviewed at an organization called Project Harmony. This was a child advocacy and support center. An organization in Nebraska that focused on helping children and families impacted by abuse, neglect, or trauma. A place where children do not have to repeat their story to multiple agencies. A safe, supportive space.

I was devastated, confused, and angry. In those moments of crisis, you never know what choices you'll make until you're forced to make them. Looking back now, I understand my state of mind at the time, but it doesn't excuse what happened next. I still loved him. How could I still love him? I still wanted my marriage to work. I wanted a family, the very thing I had been denied growing up. That desire twisted into something I can only describe as developing positive feelings toward the abuser out of a desperate need to be loved.

Later in life, and after many months of therapy, I fully understood the manipulation I was under and how my choices affected my family. Loving him did not mean I loved my daughter any less, but it meant I betrayed her while trying to save my marriage. That is something I will always regret. Over time, I transmuted that pain into something stronger. Today, nothing will ever come between the relationship I have mended and built with my daughter.

On New Year's Eve of the same year, my family received news that the youngest of my first cousins had apparently passed away in a house fire. We were all shocked, taken aback, and left feeling dismantled by the sudden impact of the information. I was devastated. How could this be? He didn't deserve to go out in flames and terror. He was only twenty years old, with a whole life ahead of him. He was everyone's favorite cousin, even my kids.

It's assumed that he may have been involved in running drugs, or something to do with that sort of lifestyle. We all had our own assumptions that maybe one thing led to another, and he ended up in some sort of trouble, with nowhere to turn. His car was found outside of a hoarder's home that burned down with his keys on the dashboard. They never found any evidence that his body was in the fire, and there were no dental records. A test for the presence of mitochondrial DNA came back negative and inconclusive, which alarmed us all and raised questions about whether this was even real. Was he really dead? Was he ever there? What really happened? We still don't know the truth, and the case is unresolved to this day.

Ten days after he passed away, his mom, my aunt, passed away too. We believe she was heartbroken to her core and died of a broken heart. The pain was too much for her physical body to handle; she searched relentlessly for answers and still came up with nothing. She died on my son's birthday. His sister, my oldest first cousin, was shunned from her family after the death of her mom and brother. Her oldest brother still has nothing to do with her today, and neither does her own father. It still majorly affects her, and she is still trying to pick up the pieces of a broken family.

While dealing with the catastrophic circumstances that death brings, not only did I have to carry that, but I also had to face what was going on in my own home. It was raw and unbelievable that this was actually happening. I had to endure not only what was taking place underneath my own roof, but also watch two of my closest family members pass ten days apart. My entire family was grieving, and it was one of the hardest moments we had to deal with.

My daughter never wanted to attend family counseling. I forced her to go so my family could stay together. I did not understand back then that I was hurting her because of the manipulation and the strong hold it had on me, in turn I manipulated her by framing the situation as a normal bump in the road that could be polished over. I did not put her first, and it has been one of the hardest mistakes I've ever had to face. In March of 2013, he was only charged with third-degree sexual assault on a minor and given five years' probation. He had to register as a sex offender for twenty five years and could not live at our house.

My best friend at the time, who I met in my early twenties, agreed to let him reside with her. He wanted to come home, but it was against his probation and the law. The night he was arrested for violating probation, he came to the house erratically and out of his mind. I kept telling him he needed to leave, reminding him he couldn't be there, but he refused and sat at the computer desk as he pulled out a gun, telling my kids and I to stay on the couch and that he wasn't going anywhere.

My best friend was there as well and called the police using the house phone without him noticing. He was sentenced to four years in prison for violating probation and possessing a weapon as a prohibited person. He fell to his knees when the cops arrived in the front yard, because he knew that he was going to face time in Nebraska State Penitentiary.

That same night, during all of the havoc, he implied that he slept with my best friend while she was sitting in the chair. I immediately looked over to her, and she had no defense. That is when I knew that my intuition was right all along. It all made sense; the dots were connecting. The nights they wouldn't want me to come to her apartment to visit, or the sly comments about their connection. I knew something wasn't right, but I was stuck in my own illusions of how I wanted the reality to be.

While he was in prison, I was a single mother, even though it wasn't on paper. I was doing normal everyday activities, still getting up and going to work, making sure my kids were doing well in school, cooking dinner every night, and keeping a clean home. I was also finally getting ready to graduate from college with my bachelor's degree in business management. I graduated from college in 2015. Even after everything happened, I was the first in my family to earn a college degree. This gave me hope. I was inspired and knew I had a purpose, regardless of life's challenges.

April 2, 2016. On my birthday, my grandmother died. This was the breaking point, a pivotal moment that caused my family to split in two. There was unequal grief, emotional intensity, changes in the family dynamic, and overall dysfunction. Our family became rivals, and when it came down to it, it was all over money and greed.

My grandmother was the backbone of our entire family on all sides, as grandmothers tend to be. We would spend holidays at her house, have summer visits, swim at the Aquacourt, and swing at the parks and recreations, visiting the Kool-Aid museum (Hastings, Nebraska, is the birthplace of the classic soft drink) and soak up all of her wisdom and love as if we were sponges, childhood memories at the lake and at the bowling alley. I can still feel the sun on my face, the warmth of its rays mixing with the cool solace of the water against my skin. The smell of popcorn and polish mingled in the air, neon lights flickering across the glossy lanes.

A place where laughter was constant and everyone felt close, connected in the simplicity of a shared game. She had Vietnamese friends who lived down the road that we would go visit, and never forget her kitchen table. That is where the good times were had, the late-night card games, the long talks, and her menthol Salem cigarettes, along with her Miller Highlife beer in the glass bottle to be exact, the champagne of beers.

Her house was the go-to place when someone needed to talk or simply to be. She was everything. She worked hard her entire life, and her decisions were always final. During her final days on this earth, true colors began to show. She was terminally ill in the hospital with pancreatic cancer, and my mom was there with her every step of the way, being her only daughter left after my aunt's death. When the doctor and nurses came to the conclusion that there was nothing else they could do, they decided it was best for her to spend her final time being alive in the comfort of her own home. The only thing my second-oldest first cousin (the middle brother) had to say was, "Well, how long does she have?"

This rubbed my mom the wrong way on many different levels. Instead of having decency and compassion for his own grandmother's pain, all he could think of was what was to come after.  My mother was hurt and disappointed. During the trips back and forth from Hastings to Omaha, all he could do was argue and belittle my mom about why the executive of will had changed from his dad to my grandmother's sister. His mother had passed, so why would she leave it to a man who was married into the family, instead of her own blood? Common sense, you would think?

My mom knew all along that it was all about the money. We will never forget, after she took her last breath, how they cracked open beers, her beers at that, at her kitchen table, and stated - "It's about time." They treated that moment as some sort of celebration rather than a loss of our family's monarchy. They looked forward to the fortune. Come to find out, after she passed, she had forgotten to remove my uncle's name from the deed of the house, and so, my mom felt like she had no time to cherish the memories within the walls of her mother's home.

With my grandma being so sick, it was one of those things that slipped through the cracks. She was now faced with splitting her own mother's home fifty - fifty with a man who not only cheated on her sister but was only in it for the money. After spending thirty four years married to my moms sister, he didn't even have the nerve to attend the funeral of the woman he once called Mother-in-Law. She was nothing but open-armed and welcoming to him being part of our family. Little does he know, the reason she removed him from the executive of the will was over the five thousand dollars she provided to him to redo her daughters' and his kitchen. He couldn't account for the last two to three thousand dollars of the money that she gave him.

Their home sat undone for twelve years while my aunt was alive, and it was one of the only things she ever wanted. After her passing, we found it funny that he was able to complete the reconstruction with the money he got from my grandmother's inheritance. Now he is remarried and living "happily ever after." This isn't a fairy tale with perfect days or endless bliss. To me, love is the ability to love without expectation, and the courage to build a life aligned with one's truth. Truth that he never shared. My Aunt died and he moved on like the life they shared was nothing to him. I think he will have to question the rest of his life.

When money is involved in a family passing, it can be heart-wrenching. It stirred up long-buried intentions rooted in our family. While it should've represented love and acknowledgment, it triggered resentment and treachery. It shouldn't be about who deserves what, but about what that person truly wanted.

It is something I never want to go through again. I have gained wisdom as I have gotten older and realized wealth does not come from money alone. Wealth and happiness come from those you love and the small, fleeting moments in life: the memories we hold and the ones we once had in our lives. My grandmother is with me every day and is one of my greatest ancestors. She guides and stands beside me in more ways than I will ever know. I believe with my whole heart she is one of the reasons I'm writing this book.

After dealing with my grandmother's passing, my husband was released in June of 2017, he came back home, and in allowing that, I betrayed my daughter once again. Her foundation of trust was shattered, and emotional distance developed. She held back, was guarded, and experienced confusion, disappointment, and anger. She confided in me years later, that in the months leading up to his release she couldn't even fathom eating because of the ache consuming her body, mind, and spirit. It was a very grueling season to go through.

All of the counseling we went through allowed us to create a safety plan to be put in place so he could reside in the household with minors. She begged me to get a divorce, crying to me, writing letters, attempting to get me to understand how she felt. She just wanted to feel seen and loved, too. She wanted me to choose her.

I was so lost in the illusion that I did not listen to her; she was fifteen at the time, and she hated me. She felt deeply rejected and backstabbed. After realizing that I was stuck in my ways, she made the decision to move out and went to live with my mother for eight months, cutting me off completely in the process. She didn't want to be there when he came back. I lost my daughter, friends, and myself; it's something I will never be proud of.

Even after his release, he went straight back to his old patterns, drugs, selling, cheating, hotels, and lies. It destroyed the hope I had been clinging onto for the past four years, and made the void of missing my daughter even greater. There was melancholy that lived inside me, that was oceans deep.

One night, after I took a shower, I went to our room in the basement and something told me to look underneath our box spring. What I found was an Altoid tin can that was filled with crystal meth. I immediately put it in my pocket and waited for my other two kids to go to bed. When they finally drifted off to sleep, there was a huge argument between him and when I confronted him. He pushed me to the ground and demanded the drugs back. I was so terrified, because I didn't know what he was capable of.

Another day, I was doing laundry and noticed the closet door was open. I went to shut it when a bag of needles fell onto the floor. I begged him to stop, so we could have the life I had been wanting for so long, but he wouldn't. I had cameras in the house, and would catch him shooting up with a belt around his arm while I sat behind my desk at work. I would come home and find she-male porn on his phone and laptop, and was disgusted. It made me question if he was sleeping with men, in return, constantly getting checked for STDs. It was nightmarish.

I lived in a constant state of fight-or-flight, dreadful of what would happen next. He was arrested again in December 2017, not even six months after his release. I will never forget when the attorney handed me the papers. I read the entire thing, and he had a sixteen year old runaway girl with him, paraphernalia, and a gun the night he got caught at the casino.

I finally realized something had to change. That's when my reality shifted. I couldn't keep living in patterns that were hurting the people I loved most. I had to put my life back together, piece by piece, and that began with acknowledging the pain I had caused; every interaction carried the weight of the past. I had to show my daughter consistently that I could protect her heart, that her feelings mattered, and that I was committed to being a mother she could depend on. Some days, I felt the weight of the shame so heavily that it was hard to keep going. I kept thinking of the ways I had failed not only her but also my other two children. Filing for divorce was just the first step; the real work was learning how to be present, accountable, and trustworthy in her life again.

Rebuilding her trust did not happen overnight. Every conversation, every interaction, I had to prove that healing our relationship wasn't just about words, it was about actions, and showing up for her again and again, that I could learn, grow, and honor her in ways I hadn't before. Now, when I look at my daughter, I see a connection that is deeper and more honest than ever before. The pain of the past hasn't disappeared, but it has been transformed into understanding, compassion, and a commitment to show up fully. What we have built is authentic, raw, and real, but it is ours.

God restored and gave me grace when I did not deserve it. It took a lot to forgive myself. I prayed many nights for God's forgiveness and compassion. It has not been easy, but there is a light at the end of the tunnel if you are willing to be accountable and do the inner work. I never deserved her forgiveness, and still don't, but I prove every day to her that I will never make that choice again. That's when God moved me to a different state. I did not write this book to bring others down. I write it to share my experience, to show that even in the deepest pain, there can be hope. What I did not know at the time was that the world is a mirror, reflecting what we put out.

*"Cheating and lying aren't struggles;
they're reasons to break up."*

*~Patti Callahan Henry*

# The Friend I Thought I knew.

There was a woman I once knew, someone I met in my early twenties, someone I had in my life for nearly 15 years. A friend I cherished, trusted, and believed I could always depend on. Someone I could rely on to keep my secrets, have my back, understand my feelings, and be a safe place to be myself. What I didn't know at the time was that this friendship would eventually shatter my understanding of loyalty, honesty, and boundaries.

We met at a telemarketing job, one of those dead-end places you land at when you're young and unsure of your next move after high school. In hindsight, the job wasn't much, but God had a purpose. We bonded quickly and became close, confiding in each other about life, love, and all the pandemonium in between.

Something about her drew me in. There was a darkness in her, and I felt compelled to help her find the light. I invited her to church, trying to fill the lonely and lost look I could see in her eyes. Looking back now, I question her intentions. Did she join the church just to belong? Just to be near me? Energy vampires are real. She quickly became a dedicated member, far more involved than I ever expected. As I began to fade away from religion, she clung to it tightly. It seemed as if when I went through the adoption, our relationship began to fade, almost like she was judging me right along with the church.

We were constantly involved in events, planning, volunteering, and acting like sisters. She practically lived with us, reading stories to my kids at night, attending family functions, meeting my grandmother, and even joining us on vacations. My mom loved her too. She was family.

In 2008 when I reconnected with the man who would eventually become my husband, who molested my daughter. Around that time, she met someone as well, my mom's fiancé's brother. I had a bad feeling, but I was too distracted by my own relationship and my slow exit from the church to notice the red flags. He was bad news. A career criminal, a master manipulator, and eventually, someone she would stab with a pair of scissors. That relationship spiraled, and she began slipping into alcoholism. She tried to bounce back, but life kept pulling her under.

At the same time, I was dealing with my own crisis, discovering that my husband had molested my daughter. With nowhere for him to go, I made the unthinkable decision to let her take him in. My best friend, the same one who was already struggling with her own issues. I thought she could help, or at least give him a place to land temporarily. That decision inevitably turned into a nightmare. He turned her apartment into a trap house, selling drugs, inviting mayhem, and dragging her deeper into addiction. It was a filthy environment, with roaches, soiled clothes everywhere, and unwashed dishes piled up.

I began to question both of them. Could I trust her? Could I even trust my husband? It felt like everything was falling apart, and I was losing control. Who was I kidding? After everything my husband had already put me through, I was still choosing something meaningless and foolish, attracting the same in return.

I questioned everything. My intuition remembered what my heart was trying to forget. Patterns repeated, even if the faces or circumstances shifted slightly. Trust had already been broken, and once that fracture existed, my mind kept revisiting it, trying to make sense of what did not add up. Part of me knew that I deserved more, even if another part of me was still trying to hold on. I didn't re-question things that felt safe. I would revisit what felt off, what felt unfinished, what never truly healed.

One of the hardest lessons I've ever had to learn is that we can only control ourselves. Not others. Not their choices. Not their cacodemons. Only our reactions, our thoughts, and how we choose to move forward.

I will never fully know everything that happened during that dark period, but I do know, without question, that she slept with my mom's fiancé. My stepdad. The man who had been in our lives since my oldest was three years old. That betrayal hit like a freight train. My mom cut ties with him, and I cut ties with her.

The day I found out, my husband told me that he caught her and my mom's fiancé kissing in the backyard. He begged my husband not to say anything and blackmailed him. He wouldn't tell me that he was still using drugs if he didn't tell my mom that they were having an affair. They would sneak off to hotels, while my mom was in the dark about it all. He told me anyway and thought the whole thing was hilarious, without regard for how this news would have another ripple effect on our family.

I immediately knew I had to tell my mom, even though it would be detrimental to her well-being. The day she found out, my oldest had a talent show. We watched her dance to Montell Jordan's "This is How We Do It". Afterward, we all packed into the car, and my mom drove us over to her apartment at the time. I didn't know she planned to beat the door down if she wasn't going to come outside. After this situation came about, we ended up finding out that she was also acquainted with the robbery at my mom's apartment, a few years prior. My mom's fiancée, his brother, and her were all involved.

While she pretended to be my friend, she was wearing my mom's jewelry and perfume, stealing gift cards out of my house, all the while sleeping with her fiancé, and possibly my husband. She and I stopped talking. For years, we barely spoke. When my husband was released from prison in June 2017, her and I were not friends. It wasn't just betrayal; it was a violation on every level of what she put us through. Family. Loyalty. Trust. All blurred into something I could not recognize anymore.

There was a mix of anger and disbelief that never fully settled. I told myself I didn't need answers, that cutting her off was enough, but deep down, some questions never stopped resurfacing. How could she cross lines like that? How could the people closest to me move without any regard for me? It's something I still question, but understand it's not meant for me to figure out.

Maybe silence was easier for her. Maybe facing me meant facing what she did, and that kind of truth isn't easy to sit with. Maybe she justified it and rewrote the story in her mind to make it easier to live with. Maybe she felt nothing at all. Silence doesn't always mean peace. Sometimes it means avoidance. Sometimes it means running from accountability, but sometimes it's the closure you need.

She ended up reaching out, wanting to talk and perhaps reconcile the years of friendship we shared. We were both hesitant, but I gave in to the idea of allowing her back into my life, leaving the past in the past. We slowly reconnected, which eventually led her to tell my mom the truth. However, she never admitted to sleeping with my husband, even though he told me.

While I was preparing to file for divorce, she began dating a man in Tennessee. I didn't know much about him at first, but she was constantly on the phone with him, on my porch, in my home, during family events. I thought it was cute. She seemed happy. She deserved love. She had a glow about her that I had never seen before. I thought that maybe this was it, just maybe she would finally be able to establish a healthy relationship that she so desperately wanted.

During this time, I was finally healing and felt so free. I was in the best state of mind I had been in a long time; I was filing for divorce, single after so many years of being bound to a toxic relationship. I was mending my relationship with my daughter. We were finally laughing and growing together again. I was working on my physical, mental, and spiritual health. I had a great job and was financially stable.

We were hanging out more than ever, and she was at my house every weekend, if not during the week. At the time, she was living with her mom to help care for her, and sometimes needed a break. What I did not like was the fact that she drank every time she was around, and it became a habit. It was the kind of drunkenness that was depressing and low vibrational. She would cry all the time and spend hours on the phone. She would be so inebriated that she would not be able to speak.

Once, I had to break down my bathroom door to find her passed out on the toilet, bleeding through her clothes, unconscious. My daughter had to help me carry her out, and still, she kept drinking and kept wallowing on the phone. I did not know then that they were constantly breaking up and getting back together, along with talking about me. She would say hateful things behind my back while sharing holidays, meals, and vacations with my family.

In August of 2018, she planned a trip to Tennessee to finally meet him. She drove there alone, stayed in a hotel, and, because she wasn't drinking, went into detox while she was visiting him. That knowledge came from him. Along with not being able to stand her the whole week she was there, or the description of not even wanting to sleep with her, but he felt bad for her. When she returned, she was glowing. They were planning to get married on Halloween in October, and he wanted to know more about her past. That's when things took another turn.

She told me he wanted to know more about her family and friends and that he was going to send me a friend request on Facebook. At the time, I didn't find it odd; I would want to know the same. One night, while she was drinking, he began asking questions about her history. She didn't want to tell him the truth about her past relationships, her drinking, the things she was hiding. So she told him, "Ask her." Meaning me.

The week before, he had sent me that friend request on Facebook. At the time, I thought it was harmless, just someone trying to get to know his future wife's best friend, but then he called me. The call was unexpected, and I was hesitant to answer at all. She told me to answer, so I did. While she was drunk upstairs, I pressed the green button. "Someone's going to tell me the fucking truth." It was the first thing I heard him say. I asked about what, he clarified, and I told him the truth. She had permitted me to be honest, and I was. I told him about the drugs, the trap house, the stabbing, and the affair with my mom's fiancé, along with the robbery. I laid it all out on the table, and I didn't feel guilty. The truth is the truth.

What I didn't expect was that it would end their relationship and completely change the direction of my own life. I would eventually move to TN, fifteen months later, and start a new life. After that conversation, he and I began talking regularly. What started as a friendship turned into something more that was unintended. I told her that he and I were talking, and that became the end of our friendship for good. We began to develop feelings for each other, and that changed everything. It was messy, but it also opened the door to healing I didn't know I needed.

*"It's all fun and games until someone gets hurt."*

*~Unknown*

# Him

Greta Garbo. Flesh and the Devil (Brown,1926). The scene in the church during communion. She gracefully took the chalice he just drank from, caressed it, and then sucked the same spot. It's profane, but it's pure. A love so desperate, it's obscene. A love so intense that it makes other people uncomfortable. That is what we had, a forbidden love.

Where do I begin? Perhaps with the unexpected visit of love that peeled away every trace of my pretentiousness. My **** Flame. I used to want to elaborate on everything we went through, but I realized, none of that matters. All that matters are three things: What I meant to him, what he meant to me, and the truth. I have to be careful with this part. I want to say everything I felt. I need you, my reader, to feel it.

To sit in the pain and feel how raw it was. How it dismantled me, how I would stay up late at night, in a panic, trying to regulate my nervous system. How I would sob myself to sleep on the couch and wake with a swollen face every night for 4 months. The flashbacks, the memories. The dreams of growing old together, of a thousand years. "*Whatever our souls are made of, his and mine are the same.*" Bronte, E. J. (1847) Wuthering Heights. Thomas Cautley Newby. My "*Damon*" Williamson. K. & Plec. J (2009, Sept) Vampire Diaries. If you know, you know.

The void I needed a connection with, and then, the moment I realized I had to let him go. The moment I understood: There was no going back. The duplicity that shook my soul. The person who knew my past and everything I went through, and the years of love I gave so freely with the purest of intentions, and a taintless heart. The loyalty, even when I knew deep down I couldn't trust him and God, I wanted to, I wanted so badly to trust him. All I wanted was union, growth, something real, and more than anything, consistency. I desperately wanted our connection to stay intact.

I remember staring at my phone, rereading old messages like they still meant something. Scrolling back to the days when everything felt easy. When consistency didn't have to be questioned. Then, looking at the present hours turning into days, months without a word. Conversations that felt forced. Energy that no longer matched what we once had. I would tell myself, just give it time. So I did.

From the start, I put my all into imagining what our life could look like together. The life we talked about for hours and hours, at a time, through long-distance phone calls for a year. After my divorce was finalized and our family was turning a new page, we decided to start a new life in Florida with my mom. Return to the place where I was originally born, Pensacola.

My goal was clear: to help my mom transition to the Gulf of Mexico, while knowing that wasn't my final destination. I was looking forward to all the things we promised each other about our future in West Tennessee, the late-night conversations about our life together. Once we were finally together. We would build, grow, and start a new chapter.

The move from Nebraska to Florida in May of 2019 was quick. In a matter of months, my home, along with my mother's,was stacked with boxes and totes, all ready to be shipped 895 miles away. We were all excited and weary of the unknown, but knew that what we were leaving behind was for the best. That chapter was closed.

The move wasn't fully planned and was intense for many different reasons. We didn't have a place set up for any of us to live, so we stayed in an extended-stay hotel for the entire summer. We were all going through the motions, just having left everything we've ever known behind and now in a new place, with no real blueprint, but the expectations of a serene horizon.

No one said what was really going on, but it was there, thick, unspoken, pressing in from every side. There were good times and bad times. There were arguments when there should have been empathy and communication. I traveled with my kids back and forth from Omaha to Tennessee, and then Pensacola a few times over that summer and early fall, while he still provided optimism about what things would be like when I finally got to him. We lived in Pensacola for a total of nine and a half months, leaving the crystal blue waters and green palm trees behind, for the tall Cypress trees of West Tennessee.

I moved across multiple state lines in the hope of something we both acknowledged, despite the back-and-forth in the relationship. The breaking up and getting back together. He knew my intentions from the beginning, and everything I wanted. We moved into a quiet, rural area, into a four-bedroom ranch-style home in a town with one gas station and one pump, a complete 360 from inner-city life.

The cultural difference was shocking and hard to swallow, but we would come to find out it was everything we needed at the time, after our hectic past. We went from below-zero weather, with 6-foot-plus of snow, to 70-degree days in January. From a population of six hundred thousand people to one thousand people. From the Great Plains to cotton fields. From midwestern food to southern barbecue, from "Fuck you, get out of the way!" to waving at strangers driving by. From a fast-paced life, having everything you need at your disposal, to having to drive thirty minutes to an hour away to the closest Walmart… talk about culture shock.

Culture shock hits you slowly, like a wave you didn't see coming. At first, it's little things, words that don't mean what you think, gestures that feel unfamiliar, routines that suddenly seem complicated. You can't help but compare everything to what you knew: the food, the smells, the sounds. The familiar comforts that once grounded you feel far away, almost unreal.

Within the first month, he moved out of his mom's and moved his belongings into our home. Little did I know at the time that I was going to be grappling with another partner facing his own addiction to alcoholism. His forte was Jack Daniel's honey-flavored whiskey, four or more at a time in the mini bottles. During our entire relationship, he was sober for maybe five months nonconsecutively. There were nights I would carry him inside because he was too drunk to stand. The slurring, the lashing out, and then nights he would be a happy, hugging, and loving drunk. That night, he pushed me to the bed and told me to stab him with his own knife. He woke up the next morning and apologized for the hundredth time, but there was never any change. It takes me back to the classic saying, actions speak louder than words.

The night I drove him to the hospital because his nephew crashed his face for being disrespectful to me. The time he yelled so violently at my ten-year-old, she was so frightened and told her counselor at school, and CPS showed up at our door; his niece and nephews were present. He had to take an online class to reflect his changed behavior. The nights he would slam my doors and start fights and argue with me because he was drinking, the hole he put in my bedroom door, or the hole in the kitchen wall.

The constant calls to his family when disagreements broke out, and his mom had to calm him down. The time his mom locked herself in the bathroom, because he was drinking and went into rage mode. The night he grabbed me by the neck as I was trying to walk out the back door. His defense was that he was trying to keep me safe.

It was a constant hot and cold in the relationship, which left me emotionally unstable. I thought if I could hold on long enough, he would see my value and prioritize our future, but instead, I was met with questions about my worth and constant ghosting whenever I expressed my feelings. Who was there to take him to rehab? After everything was said and done, I was told I was never there for him.

The times he would go to the bar and not tell me, the inconsistent behavior. I felt like the third wheel when his friends were around, rather than his partner. "Two against the world." He would express. The time he lied to me about going to a hotel, and specifically told me there was another woman there, along with his best friend and his partner. How could he think I would be comfortable with that, even if he said "I didn't sleep with her."? Manipulation at its finest. He made me question everything.

Recovering from betrayal is one of the hardest things you'll ever face. I had to grieve the idea of him. I had to mourn the man I believed him to be, because the very person who was supposed to be my comfort, my safety, my sanctuary, was the one who tore me apart. He became the source of my trauma. Partner backstabbing is real. I trusted him with my heart, and he handed it back bloodied and broken.

I carried the cracks of his choices like they were my own, not realizing they belonged to him alone. It wasn't because of a flaw in me, but a reflection of his character. His choices. His inability to honor, respect, or remain loyal. No amount of love, patience, or effort on my part could change that. No amount of "being better" could rewrite the story he was already living. I understand that because I kept choosing him after everything he put me through, I was mirroring back to the universe what I was willing to accept. It was not all his fault, although he will say it's all mine. He loved me the best he knew how and I will always be grateful for that experience. Our good times were really good, but our bad times were just as bad.

I thought I wasn't enough, but it wasn't about that. When someone shows they cannot hold space for you, when they cannot show up, when they cannot carry what the relationship requires, it is simply because they don't have the capacity. The mornings when I would stare at his beautiful face, run my fingers across his eyebrows, whisper in his ears, and put my finger in his belly button. I wanted him to run back and confess he was sorry, that he would never do it again. To say we'd grow old and be happy together, while sitting on our porch swing with coffee.

It was divine, and it destroyed me, but he couldn't do the work. He chose distractions and other women, easy escapes, instead of the deep healing that love requires. He chose to fill the void with another body rather than work on himself and heal.

April 7th, 2025, the day he broke up with me, five days after my birthday, which he forgot. I saw it in his face. Smelled the perfidy in his aura. I knew he was cheating. I couldn't prove it, but I could sense it. Call it instinct, an animal thing. Wink, wink.

All the years of the back and forth, and I could finally see it. We had spent three weeks apart. The last argument was about the car. He wanted to use it for work, while I was starting a new job and  holding down a household. I was drowning, and still trying to help him every way I could. When I said no, he told me I wasn't supportive. The car needed a timing belt, and I was scared to let it be driven around, knowing the work that would be required.

In the car, in his mom's driveway, while breaking up with me, I fidgeted. That's when he said, "That's how I know you're full of shit." He didn't even realize I was having a panic attack. He was dumping me, and I shut down. I couldn't speak. I had no words, and I was frantic. Paralyzed, abandoned. Again.

May 2025 was the beginning of the grief. Three weeks after the breakup, he asked me what I wanted. I said, "I want us to work on ourselves. I want to come back together, healed." Friday, May 2nd - I saw him in the Walmart parking lot, putting groceries in another woman's car. He seemed so unbothered, like he hadn't shattered my world. He defended her when I confronted them. When I asked her if she knew who I was, she said, "Yes. He told me about you."

I left Walmart without my groceries. I was hysterical and dysregulated, crushed. I cried my entire journey home. I had just started a new job, and I was going through the worst heartbreak of my life.

All of May, I was a ghost. I crashed out, wept, and felt as though the floor beneath me had disappeared. The grief was relentless, and heavy, pressing down on every part of me. I begged for answers, not just why this had happened, but why I had been left to navigate the chaos alone. I reached out to his friends, his family, anyone who might understand, anyone who could give me a sliver of clarity.

Instead, I was mocked, ridiculed, and turned into a joke on Facebook, as if my pain and confusion were nothing more than entertainment. His entire family seemed to delight in labeling me "crazy", twisting my heartbreak into gossip. Every post, every shared message in their clan chat, every comment and shared laugh felt like a knife in my chest, cutting deeper than the original wound.

I remember scrolling through, frozen, and shaking, feeling exposed, humiliated, and utterly alone. The people I had hoped would understand or at least respect my grief were now part of the chorus that dismissed it. It wasn't just the embarrassment; it was the message behind it: that my truth didn't matter, that my feelings were invalid, and that the very real pain I was carrying could be weaponized against me. The last 7 years meant nothing and I was so easily disposed of.

I gave this man seven years of my life. His family completely enabled his narrative, and instead of showing kindness and compassion, I was met with hate. The profile stalking and flipped narrative, like I was the one stalking him when in reality they would both watch me from afar. The only message I ever received from him was that she did not know about his account he created on Tik Tok and he could not face his own feelings. He would post indiscrete messages about missing his ex, and that he thought about me all the time. It was confusing, and manipulation. The same marriage date they have, that we had for years, that his ex and him had before us. It's crazy to think about now. The same necklace she wore was around my neck for 7 years. He constantly blamed his autism for his behavior, yet he was never diagnosed. Although I saw the signs, it never gave him the right to treat people like shit.

Let's not forget, he took her to his mother's house for Mother's Day. I had just been there three weeks prior, celebrating his niece and nephew's birthdays. The blows didn't stop, but eventually, something shifted. Yes, I grieved, every memory, every touch, every kiss, every time we made love.

I danced alone in the kitchen and could feel the echo of his ghost, but I had to let the memories stay, not to torture myself, but to remember what I survived. To remember what I learned. I would not be the woman I am now if I hadn't loved him. I would not be the woman I am now if I hadn't lost him.

We don't move on from people. We move forward with them. They come with us, in every decision, every moment, every new love. He is part of me, always, but the version of me he knew? She no longer exists. I'm stronger, wiser, more intense, more whole, more radiant, more aligned, and finally, more me.

This heartbreak changed everything, and it made life more sacred. Now, I see the world through a different lens. Love is always bigger than hate. Compassion is always louder than judgment, and when you live a life you love, love shows up in the most unexpected of ways. I still hold his memory and hope one day he knows that the only thing I ever wanted was growth. You do not choose a relationship for worth; you choose a relationship for growth.

I wanted him to stop confusing accountability with blame. He would go quite the second I asked a question that mattered. Not loud, not angry, just a shift. A wall sliding into place where openness should have been. The moment I wanted to understand was the moment everything twisted.

A sharp two edged sword where there didn't need to be one. I'd pause, blinking, trying to find where the conversation slipped out of my hands, but it didn't matter what I said. He was already somewhere else, defending, deflecting, rewriting. What started as reaching for clarity always turned into me explaining myself. " I'm not blaming you," I'd whisper. "I just… need you to see it." He never stayed long enough in the moment to look. Every question became an attack. Every feeling I had became something he had to escape, not only from him, but his family as well.

I'm not sure if we will ever talk again. I pray that one day he can be accountable and that one day we can have that conversation, even if we are not together. That he can heal and break his own cycles of fear, abandonment, and avoidant cycles. I hope that one day he can be the best man he can be. He has so much potential, and I wanted that for us, for myself, for him, for our once upon a time family.

A friend asked me once if it was really love. I told her it absolutely was. It had to be him; he was the one that I needed. He showed me how to love myself on such a deep level that it awakened my soul. Although we did not make it and he was my almost, he awakened something in me that I will forever be grateful for. He helped me look at the cycles I needed to break and the versions of myself that no longer aligned with my soul.

No one else can build a life on another woman's tears and call it theirs. I've learned this the hard way. Happiness, love, and trust are not trophies to be won by stepping over someone else's heart. Any life constructed on betrayal is fragile, hollow, surface-level, and destined to repeat the same patterns. I've come to see that his choices were not about me or about the other woman; they were about a pattern he carried, a way of avoiding accountability, of seeking fulfillment in shortcuts that were ultimately taught to him by his family and will leave pain in their wake. The cycle of betrayal doesn't disappear simply because a new partner enters the picture; the underlying habits and disregard for the consequences of his actions will continue to follow him.

This realization became liberation. I understood that her presence, her triumph, did not diminish my worth. I would not be the collateral damage in someone else's story. Their temporary happiness, built on the same patterns that caused me so much pain, could never hold depth, honesty, or integrity that I was now reclaiming for myself.

True healing, real life, and meaningful love cannot exist on deception or exploitation. That truth freed me to stop looking outward and start rebuilding my life from a foundation of respect, accountability, and self-love.

It really is bittersweet, but so damn beautiful. I will always carry him with me and love him. That love will always have a profound impact on me.

There is not a day that goes by that I don't think about him, but deep down, I know that I have to move forward. I have learned that the universe works in mysterious ways, and I know without a doubt we were meant to cross paths. I have transmuted the hurt, anger, and bitterness into something beautiful, and he was the catalyst to my growth. The long journey to Tennessee has influenced so much of my life, and I will forever be grateful for that.

I have no regrets and will always think of our time together with luminosity and rarity. There is no hate in my heart for what has happened, but a profound knowledge that

# PART II

# *Acceptance*

Accepting the process is like accepting the thorns on a rose bush; you bleed, but you also recognize the beauty in the bloom. When we're children, we grow by learning. As adults, we learn by surviving. Some of us carry the weight of choices we didn't even fully understand when we made them. But the goal, always, is to learn from the past so we don't repeat it. You have to take a hard look in the mirror. Really look. You have to drag yourself out of the tar pit you created and begin to heal.

Acceptance resonates with truth, especially the ugly truths. And once you do that, your perception begins to shift. You start to see the life you've lived and the life you have the power to create. Now that you've read the introduction and understand the life I've lived, the pain, the betrayals, the raw humanity of it all, I want to show you how I began to overcome it, how I aligned with purpose, with God, and with my faith. Acceptance isn't just the first step; it's the key. It forces you to reflect. To realign. To come back to the center. To breathe peace into the chaos.

Once you accept the pain, the fog begins to lift. You find clarity. You place one foot in front of the other. You start a whole new journey. And it won't be easy. It'll humble you, but it will be worth it. Like a mosaic, once broken, you can rebuild it into something even more breathtaking. You have to give yourself time to figure out who you are. And when you do, you'll start to see what still needs healing, sometimes all the way back to childhood. What many people forget is this: when you suppress your emotions, they will surface. Maybe not today. Maybe not for years. But when they do, you'll be faced with a choice: You can transmute that energy into something beautiful. Or you can continue to feed the same old narrative.

Once I accepted who I am, flaws and all, I instantly shifted my frequency. It's like the veil drops. I looked around and realized what I have been attracted to. I'm the only one who can change it. A really good friend once told me, "Stop trying to fill the void, and allow the void to consume you." What she said stopped me in my tracks. It helped me overcome the hardest lesson of my life. It allowed me to fully embrace the present and let go of everything I could not control.

You have to learn to love yourself. I'm not talking about spa days or bubble baths, though that's part of it. I'm talking about the real work: The shadow work. Self-reflection. The uncomfortable conversations with your own soul. Acceptance isn't easy. But I swear to you, it leads to a peace so profound, so undeniable, that you'll never go back. There are endless benefits to self-acceptance. When we step into our true selves, we become empowered in ways that shake the earth beneath us. We start to see clearly for the first time. To live life fully, you have to know who you are. To know who you are, you have to accept who you've been.

When we begin to accept ourselves, we stop resisting our humanity. We stop rejecting our scars and our struggles. Instead, we begin to find security and liberation. We realize that most of our self-rejection stems from fear, fear planted in us by trauma, upbringing, relationships, and society. And when we finally face that fear instead of running from it, it begins to lose its power over how we see ourselves. And make no mistake, lack of self-acceptance has consequences. It can touch every corner of our lives:

- Lower self-confidence
- Emotional instability
- Avoidance
- Anxiety
- Unhealthy relationships

When we don't accept ourselves, we build a life rooted in defense mechanisms rather than truth. As Vanourek (2023) puts it, these signs can become pervasive, spilling into relationships, careers, and even our health. So how do we change? Here are some practices that Vanourek (2023) describes that have helped change my life:

- Stop self-criticizing. Speak kindly to yourself. Your inner voice matters.
- Stop comparing yourself to others. You're measuring your beginning against someone else's middle or end.

- Dive inward. Unpack the guilt and shame. Trace it back. Ask yourself where it came from, and if it even belongs to you.
- Practice self-compassion. Forgive yourself for not knowing what you didn't know.
- Understand that we all learn in our own time. Your journey is uniquely yours.

As you begin practicing self-acceptance, don't forget to look outward, too. Find balance by being of service. Contribute to your community. Connect with nature. Ground yourself in creation. When you spend too much time focused on whether you're "good enough," you lose touch with what really matters: Connection. Contribution. Compassion. During my shadow work, I learned that giving back is medicine. It shifts the energy. It breaks the cycle. It helps you become whole.

Seek God, Seek the Source. Seek Mother Earth. Stand under the moon. Feel her reassurance. You are one soul on a planet of billions, yet you were placed here for a purpose. What is yours? What do you have to offer? Self-acceptance is grounding. It's not trendy. It's not surface. It's deep soul work. But when you embrace it fully, it changes everything. It changes the way you walk through the world. The way you connect, the way you love. The way you heal is one of the most worthwhile things you'll ever do. And if you're brave enough to keep walking, you'll find that life after acceptance? It's the beginning of everything.

*"When we are no longer able to change a situation, we are challenged to change ourselves."*

*~Viktor E. Frankl*

# Grace

After we accept what we've done in our lives, and take a hard, unfiltered look at where we are, we begin to experience something else entirely: grace. Not just grace for ourselves, but grace for others. We start to realize that we're all here, spinning together on this rock called Earth, and no matter how different our stories may be, we're all connected. We all bleed, we all cry, we all long for love and understanding. Just because our pain feels unique doesn't mean someone else's pain is any less valid, our perception shifts. Reality softens. We begin to see the world with more empathy, and ourselves with more truth. We stop seeing ourselves as broken. We start seeing ourselves as becoming. Accepting your current reality is often the first step toward real change. It's not surrendering, it's reclaiming.

Acceptance restores energy. It frees up space in your spirit. It gives you the capacity to move forward rather than resist what already is. And then the real question arrives: What are you going to do with all that energy? Will you transmute it into something beautiful, something grounded in purpose and growth? Or will you let it rot in the corners of your soul, turning into bitterness, self-sabotage, and more of the same? There's a moment when you have to ask yourself: "What did I learn, so I don't repeat the same cycle?" Because you will repeat it if you don't ask that question. This is radical accountability. This is where real transformation begins.

We are each responsible for our own emotional landscape. We are responsible for how we react, how we speak, how we love, and how we treat people. And that responsibility requires grace. No one comes from the exact same background. We all carry stories no one else knows. But it takes nothing to be kind to others and to ourselves. Taking ownership of your patterns, your triggers, your bad behavior, it's not a punishment. It's power. It doesn't mean you excuse what others have done to you. Their actions are their responsibility. Their hurtful choices are theirs to reckon with. But your healing? Your peace? That's on you.

When you hold yourself accountable without shame, when you own your part without making excuses, you become a version of yourself that no longer needs to chase closure or prove your worth. You just are. And that's grace. Nothing outside of you is required to validate what you've already made peace with within. A quiet, unshakable knowing that no one else gets to define anymore.

*" To write about life, first you must live it."*

*~ Ernest Hemingway*

# After Acceptance and Grace

There is a quiet moment after the storm, the moment when you've stopped fighting what is and allowing God to have control. Acceptance settles in like dusk after a long, blinding day. You stop struggling against the inevitable, stop rewriting the past in your mind, and simply allow things to be as they are. And then, from that stillness, grace appears. Grace is softer than acceptance. Acceptance says, "This is what happened." Grace whispers, "And I can love it anyway." Grace does not excuse or erase; it embraces. It makes peace with imperfection and welcomes humanity in every broken edge.

In that welcome, something begins to loosen. But what comes after that? After the surrender, the forgiveness, the loosening of your grip? What happens when the fight is over? At first… nothing. No grand revelation. No sudden transformation. Just space. A quiet you're not used to. A stillness that almost feels unfamiliar. Slowly, you begin to notice you're not carrying it the same way anymore. What once consumed you now just passes through you. The weight doesn't grip you. The story doesn't control you.

# The Season of Letting Go

I remember when everything seemed to fall apart at once. My relationship had ended, my job felt meaningless, and even my faith, once steady and sure, felt like a language I no longer spoke. For weeks, I moved through my days as though underwater, the world muffled and heavy. One morning, sitting in my car outside the grocery store, I realized I was holding on to too many things that no longer fit: the need to be right, the illusion of control, the belief that life had to unfold exactly as I planned. Tears came without ceremony. I let them. That was the first small act of acceptance.

Acceptance wasn't a grand revelation; it was a weary exhale. A quiet "Fine. This is where I am." And slowly, that acknowledgment created a little space, a breath between me and my pain. Grace came later, on an ordinary afternoon with a quickening pulse. There was nothing. Not indifference, something gentler. I saw all the people who hurt me not as the villains of my story, but as other human beings who had also been trying, failing, and learning. In that moment, I understood grace not as something earned, but as something given, freely, because we all need it.

# The Quiet Birth of Peace

After acceptance and grace, something unexpected happened. The noise inside me began to quiet. It didn't happen overnight, but over time, I noticed I could sit in silence without the constant replay of "what ifs." Peace arrived quietly, like dawn light creeping through curtains. I could still remember everything that had happened—but the memory no longer burned. It simply existed. Peace is not the absence of emotion; it's the absence of resistance. It's the steady heartbeat that says, "I can live with this. I can still live."

# Freedom: The Unseen Reward

Peace gave way to freedom. Not the kind you can see from the outside, but an inner spaciousness. I stopped checking social media for signs of how others were living. I stopped rehearsing old arguments in my mind. Freedom was realizing I could move forward without needing to rewrite the past. I could let people think what they would, and still be okay. The heavy, invisible chains of resentment fell away, one by one. Freedom is laughter returning after silence. It's walking down a familiar street without flinching at old memories. It's looking at your reflection and finally seeing yourself again. It's the great Let Them Theory of Me Robbins, which I have tattooed on my arm.

# Growth: The Quiet Bloom

When peace and freedom took root, growth began to bloom. It was subtle, so gentle that at first I didn't notice. I started saying yes to small things: dinner with friends, a new book, a morning walk. Growth didn't come from forcing change; it came from allowing life to flow again. I began to respond with patience instead of anger, curiosity instead of fear. It wasn't about becoming someone new; it was about remembering who I had always been before the pain. The same soil that had been hardened by grief became fertile ground for new things to grow.

# Love: The Circle Completed

And then, without force, without warning, love returned. Not the kind I was chasing, but the kind that was waiting inside me all along. Love for myself, for the choices I made and the ones I didn't. Love for the people who hurt me, because they taught me what I most needed to learn about forgiveness. Love for the life that didn't go as planned, but somehow still became beautiful. When you arrive at love, you realize that acceptance and grace were never the ending; they were the doorways. Love is the home you were always walking toward.

# Wisdom: The Harvest

Peace, freedom, growth, and love, these are the quiet fruits of wisdom. Wisdom doesn't come with age; it comes with surrender. It's the moment you finally understand that joy and pain are not opposites, but partners in shaping the soul. Wisdom whispers, "You are still whole, even here."And maybe that's what comes after acceptance and grace, not perfection, not certainty, but the deep knowing that whatever happens next, you can meet it with an open heart.

# Conclusion: The Gentle Turning and Alignment

Life has a way of circling back, offering us new chances to practice what we thought we had already mastered. Acceptance and grace are not singular moments of enlightenment; they are daily choices. Some days they arrive easily, like a deep breath. Other days, they ask us to lay down our pride, our control, our fear, and begin again. After we've walked through the storm—after the ache, the surrender, and the softening, we begin to notice a new rhythm forming in our lives. The breaking and the mending. The falling and the rising. Each time we return to acceptance and grace, we carry a little more wisdom, a little more gentleness, a little more truth.

What comes after acceptance and grace is not an ending. It's the quiet unfolding of peace, freedom, growth, love, and wisdom, and trusting that God has a bigger plan. It's learning to live unguarded, to hold the world, and ourselves, with open hands, and perhaps that is the quiet miracle of it all: that even after everything falls apart, something tender remains, the capacity to begin again, to trust again, to love again. When you can cut every version of yourself off that does not align with God, with the universe, you, in return, gain everything you have always wanted. The world is our mirror, and what we put out is what we will get in return. What are you willing to accept and put out into the universe? What are you mirroring back to the universe, your reality?

# Reflection and Practice

Take a few moments to sit with these questions. You might write your responses in a journal, or simply let them rest in your heart.

1. What truth in your life have you been resisting?
2. What would acceptance look like, not approval or agreement, but gentle acknowledgment?
3. Where might you offer grace?
   To yourself? To someone else? To a situation that still stings?
4. What would peace feel like in your body if you allowed it in? Imagine breathing it in, one slow inhale at a time.
5. How might you begin again, with softness, with freedom, with love?
6. What are you aligning with? What are you mirroring back to the world?

# Take Away

This book is rooted in my lived experiences, every lesson, every wound, every moment of growth. Its purpose is to remind you that your story does not end where your pain begins. You are not confined to a life shaped by trauma; you have the power to rise beyond it. This is an invitation to choose healing, to pursue wholeness, and to believe that becoming better is always within reach. Even after being deeply hurt, love is still possible. A full, meaningful life is still yours to claim. There is light, and always, on the other side of darkness. Healing is a choice we must make again and again, and love is a force we can return to, even when it feels distant. Pain may be inevitable, but suffering is not where your story has to stay. You can still choose love. In the end, that choice will always be the greatest gift you give, to yourself, and to the world.

# References

Vanourek, G. (2023, August 2). The Incredible Grounding Power of Self- Acceptance.

Gregg Vanourek Good life Good work. Retrieved from: https://greggvanourek.com/power-of-self-acceptance

Falk, D. (2023, September 25). Is Consciousness Part of the Fabric of the Universe?

Retrieved from: https://www.scientificamerican.com/article/is-consciousness-part-of-the-fabric-of-the-universe1/

Bronte, E. (1847, December). Wuthering Heights

Retrieved from: Wuthering Heights

Brayton, W. (2010, June 15). Kahlil Gibran

Retrieved from: https://allpoetry.com/column/7553497-Kahlil-Gibran--by-WandaLeaBrayton

Clifford, C. (2026). "Children are like wet cement. Whatever falls on them makes an impression". - Haim Giott

Retrieved from: https://fpa.org/children-are-like-wet-cement-whatever-falls-on-them-makes-an-impression-haim-ginott/

The Australian Financial Literacy Foundation. *The great art of learning is to understand but a little at a time*

Retrieved from: https://www.aflf.com.au/our-offering-1

Good News Network (April, 2019). Quote of the day - "Cheating and lying aren't struggles, They're reasons to break up." - Patti Callahan Henry

Retrieved from: https://www.goodnewsnetwork.org/patti-callahan-henry-quote-on-break-ups/

"It's all fun and games until someone gets hurt." (1990's). A common Idiom Warning.

Retrieved from: https://www.google.com/search?sca_esv=36815ad48fdd2e61&hl=en&gbv=2&sxsrf=ANbL-n5Bp-beMvcA2n26Zza8kfifcTe3gA%3A1777338688543&q=%E2%80%9CIt%E2%80%99s+all+fun+and+games+until+someone+gets+hurt.%E2%80%9D+&oq=%E2%80%9CIt%E2%80%99s+all+fun+and+games+until+someone+gets+hurt.%E2%80%9D+&aqs=heirloom-srp..0l5

goodreads (2026). Robert Frost Quotes

Retrieved from: https://www.goodreads.com/quotes/15633-love-is-an-irresistible-desire-to-be-irresistibly-desired

"Heart of Darkness" *Vampire Diaries*, created by Kevin Williamson & Julie PlecJulie Plec, Season 3 Episode 10, Produced for CW Network by Warner Bros Television, and Alloy Entertainment, 2012.

*Flesh and the Devil* (Brown, 1926) -The Communion Scene High Quality1080p-Youtube

Retrieved from:

https://www.youtube.com/watch?v=ugprbLfG5rU

www.ingramcontent.com/pod-product-compliance
Lightning Source LLC
Chambersburg PA
CBHW022111050726
47591CB00002B/755
*9781968092771*